THE STRUGGLE

WITH A

PURPOSE

DO YOU TRUST *WHO YOU PROFESS...*?
OR
***WHAT YOU POSSESS...*?**

LESLIE A. MCNEILL

THE STRUGGLE WITH A PURPOSE:
DO YOU TRUST WHO YOU PROFESS…? … OR
…WHAT YOU POSSESS…?

The Struggle with a Purpose: Do you trust who you profess or what you possess?

Library of Congress Control Number TXU001304809

ISBN978-1-60725-481-2

Cover Illustrated and Designed by: Tnomal Entertainment
Edited by: Mr. Michael Fairley (my cuz, cuz), Mrs. Tammie L. Cook (my sister/cuz) and Ms. Joyce Daye (my spiritual mom)

Printed by:
Laser Image Printing and Marketing
4018 Patriot Drive, Suite 200
Durham, NC 27703
www.laserimagenc.com

This Book Is Dedicated To

My Faithful Savior, Jesus Christ,

My Wonderful, Loving Husband, John (June) McNeill,

My Two Bundles of Joy, Demarius and Domineke,

My belated Mother, Laura Jacqueline (Jackie) Fairley

ENDORSEMENTS FOR

The Struggle with a Purpose: Do you trust Who you Pr*ofess* "or" What you *Possess*?

"Hey Ba"

It's an honor to have your bold outpouring spirit in my presence. I'm so proud of you. I'm proud to call you my wife because you are a very special person. Yes, I have my head up and chest out. I'm not as swift with the pen as you, but I would like to say this, when we talked about you writing your story, I thought "cool go ahead." But, I didn't know you were going to tell *ours*. But, to think where God has brought us would be selfish to keep it to ourselves. My prayer is that this book will give someone the courage to keep pressing forward. When things aren't happening in our timing, it doesn't mean that God isn't working. Buffie (Leslie), I love you and support your work 1000%. We all are waiting on the next book.

Husband, John McNeill Jr.
CEO, Asharp Production, Inc

4

Buffie (Leslie),

Your book was a testament to our childhood and survival. I am so proud of you for writing this book and telling your story. I hope that it serves as an inspiration to others. You have and always will be very special to me. I love you Sis! Continue to motivate and counsel others, you're needed. You are a wonderful example of a Godly woman.

Your lil brother,
Ricky Fairley

Leslie McNeill has been one of my most beloved and treasured friends for many years. She exemplifies a lifestyle of humility, integrity, compassion for others, and an unfailing devotion to her family and God. Her example has been a catalyst to motivate countless others to succeed in their own dreams and visions from God. The birthing of this book has come about through several devastating events. However these struggles have yielded unto her a gift of wisdom beyond her years. Leslie's life has been graciously kissed by God through His divine orchestration of trials and triumphs all of which show forth His excellent Majesty.

Therefore it is of no surprise to me that God would use his reflection of Queen Esther "for such a time as this" to reveal His plans and purposes for the lives of others. It is under the direction and leading of the Holy Spirit she has produced (The Struggle with a Purpose) a book full of inspiration and hope for the body of Christ and beyond! It is with extreme candidacy that she takes the reader on a journey with her to find God's purpose for her life. In reviewing these pages I found many inspirational points shared. First I was encouraged to know that God uses "everyday people" and often tragic circumstances as a platform for His glory. Secondly God is ultimately sovereign over every situation in our lives no matter what choices we may make. He wants to be the champion and direction for our lives. Thirdly the tremendous grace of God is demonstrated in that He gives us strength beyond human abilities. He is our source to endure and to overcome overwhelming adversities. Finally I was motivated to "trust in the Lord with all of my heart and not to lean to my own understanding" Proverbs 3:5. After reading this body of work my confidence in the Lord, Jesus Christ has been strengthened to know that God will "perfect (ALL) that concerns me" according to Psalm 138:8!

First Lady, Minister Valerie J. Jones

PREFACE

This book is about the events that happened in my life, which were stepping stones towards fulfilling God's purpose. I started pursuing God's purpose for my life in 1998. As I continued to work in corporate America, His Purpose was clearly revealed to me. I am grateful to my husband for his encouragement, patience and support. He continues to give me that extra "PUSH" to be all that God calls me to be. It is my prayer that this book will encourage you to pursue God's call for your life and allow Him to fulfill His purpose, no matter what obstacles come your way. Remember: "Trust in the Lord with all your heart; do not depend on your own understanding. Seek his will in all you do, and he will direct your paths." (Proverbs 3:5-6). "And we know that God causes everything to work together for the good of those who love God and are called according to his purpose for them." (Romans 8:28).

Get ready to be all that "God" has called *you* to be!!!!

Leslie A. McNeill

Contents

PART IV

HOW TO BE EFFECTIVE AND SUCCESSFUL IN YOUR CAREER

PART V

PROMOTION COMES FROM GOD

PART VI

TIME TO USE YOUR GOD GIVEN TALENTS/GIFTS

PART VII

FEARS THAT HINDER FULFILLING YOUR DREAM

PART VIII

THE STRUGGLE

WITH A

PURPOSE

DO YOU TRUST *WHO YOU PROFESS…*?
OR
***WHAT YOU POSSESS…*?**

LESLIE A. MCNEILL

PART 1

FINDING HOPE
AFTER PAIN

1

I LOST MY PARENTS
AT A YOUNG AGE

When I was young, I had to accept responsibilities early. My dad died in a car accident when I was two years old, and my mom died from leukemia when I was 15. I have one brother, and we were very close to our mother. Her death made our lives take a drastic turn. My mother fought leukemia for four years. During the last year of her sickness, the doctors said they could do nothing else for her, so they sent her home. As days passed, she quickly lost control of her bodily functions. When she slowly lost her speaking and walking abilities, I realized she was dying. Fear and uncertainty about my future without my mother struck me. I didn't know how I would live without her. She was like a sister, and I could talk to her like a friend. The days passed and my mom grew weaker until finally her life ended. As we prepared for her burial, we realized that she did not have a big life insurance policy; therefore, we needed all of her resources to pay for her funeral.

2

KEEPING PEACE
IN THE FAMILY

After her funeral service, I found out that my grandfather had willed the family house in which we were living and all the remaining land to my mother. So, when my mom died, there were about 53 acres of land left to my brother and I. At our age, we didn't know too much about land or its value, but we knew that granddaddy and grandmother worked hard for it. Some of our aunts and uncles approached us about the land. In fairness, they thought they should get some land as well, since it belonged to their parents. When I turned 18, we went to the courthouse and gave each child who didn't receive a portion of land the amount our aunts and uncles thought was their equal share. We could have kept it all, but in order to keep the peace, we didn't. After we divided the land, my brother and I were left with the family house and 3.5 acres each. I'm very thankful for my cousin and my aunt who lived with us. They became our guardians which kept us from having to live in a foster home or some other unfamiliar environment. They didn't have all the answers for the extra responsibilities either, but with the knowledge they had, they raised us the best they could. As I look back over my life, I realize that God was with me through it all. I gained a relationship with Him that I never knew I had until I became an adult and accepted Him into my life. As I released the deaths of my mom, my dad, and my circumstances to Him, I constantly remind myself of the scripture that says,

"And everyone who has given up houses or brothers or sisters or father or mother or children or property, for my sake, will receive a hundred times as much in return and will have eternal life." (Matthew 19:29).

That scripture gives me comfort as I think of the events that happened.

3

HELPING OTHERS
FIND HOPE

As time went on, I met people who had been through similar struggles. With compassion and encouragement, I helped them get through their struggles. We should understand that God gives us strength to go through trials so we can share our testimony with others. When others hear how we overcame our situations and circumstances, our victories give them hope so they can conquer theirs. As I look over my life, I see that God is taking me on a spiritual journey. I realize that my mother left a legacy of endurance behind for me to follow. My mother didn't go to church often, but she practiced many of God's principles in her life. Watching how she responded to hard times, difficulty, suffering, and pain taught me how to endure and persevere through my struggles. This is a good example of the most effective way to train our children. Children may not listen to everything parents say, but they will do what they see their parents do. My mom rarely ever complained, and she never gave up. She had a strength that came from within.

Notes

PART II

FINDING THE MEANING OF LIFE

1

SO WHAT NEXT?

The older I got, the more challenging my struggles became. I learned that the way I responded to those struggles determined how long they would last and what the outcome would be. This knowledge prepared me for the many chapters of life's adventure. The first part of my journey began when I prepared for college. When I enrolled in 1986, I didn't know what I wanted to study. I thought I should pursue a career that would allow me to make large amounts of money. At that time, I didn't know that God created us all to fulfill a certain purpose connected with our chosen career. So my first year in college, I enrolled with an undecided major. I didn't know what I wanted to do in life. My sophomore year I decided to major in Manufacturing Systems. I had no interest in this field, but I thought I could make large amounts of money. I wanted to major in Engineering, but I thought the courses would be too hard, so I chose the next closest field. In 1989, I accepted a Cooperative education assignment with the Federal Aviation Administration (FAA), as a Management Analyst. I also thought this experience would give me the skills to obtain a good paying job after graduation. In 1990, I finished all requirements to obtain my Manufacturing Systems degree, and an instructor advised me to take an additional 16 hours to obtain a double major in Automotive Technology or Electronics. I chose Automotive Technology, because this major would teach me the basic knowledge of a car- - but I wasn't interested in this either. However with this knowledge mechanics wouldn't cheat me when I needed to have my car serviced.

2

FINDING YOUR
DREAM JOB

Six months before graduation, I received another Cooperative assignment -- this time with the National Aeronautics and Space Administration (NASA), as a Research Assistant and I helped build a Personnel Launch System called the HL-20, which is similar to the space shuttle. I took this assignment hoping the experience would help me get a high paying job. In 1991, I graduated Cum Laude with two bachelors' degrees (Manufacturing Systems and Automotive Technology). Even though I graduated with honors, I still felt incomplete. I was happy I graduated, but I felt I wasted five years of my life pursuing degrees in subjects in which I had no interest. My focus was wrong. My college objective should have been to pursue a degree in my passion, instead of pursuing a degree in a subject that could make me the most money. We all know that no matter how much money we make, the money means nothing if we aren't happy and content. Money can't buy happiness. Only God can give us that feeling of peace, joy and contentment. Even though I thought I wasted five years of my life, God used all of what I had done for His purpose and plan for my life. We must realize that nothing happens by coincidence. God really does cause ALL things (good or bad), to work together for the good of those who love Him and are called according to His purpose.

3

SEEKING A JOB <u>YOU LOVE</u>
VS
A JOB <u>WITH A HIGH PAY STATUS</u>

After graduation I looked for a job that would pay me lots of money. With honors status, two degrees and cooperative education experience, I thought finding a good paying job wouldn't be a problem. At almost every place I applied, employers told me I was either over qualified or didn't have enough experience. I tried to convince them that I was willing to take a lower paying job to get my feet in the door and afterwards I could work my way up.

"Unless you are faithful in small matters, you won't be faithful in large ones." (Luke 16:10).

As I continued to look for a job, I finally found a company in Durham, NC, that would hire me. They hired me on first shift as a packaging inspector and paid me $6.00 per hour. I worked my way up to quality inspector, which paid $6.30 per hour. Even though my pay was much lower than I expected, I gained experience which prepared me for my next opportunity. Later I accepted a second shift job as a Motor Control Inspector, which paid $12.00 per hour. Now I was working two jobs. After about one year on my 2nd shift job, I was offered a position as Team Leader, which paid $15.00 per hour.

Notes

PART III

MY SOUL MATE

1

MARRY FOR BETTER, OR WORSE, SICKNESS OR HEALTH

In 1993, I entered the second phase of my life: Marriage.

I married "June," a guy from my home town. He knew me from my childhood days on my granddaddy's farm, and we attended school together from preschool through high school. After we married, I resigned from the quality inspector's job. In 1995, I became pregnant with my first child, and because of complications, my doctor put me on bed rest for six months. During this time I felt very helpless. The doctors instructed me not to do anything but shower and use the restroom. Since I was Mrs. "Independent," being on bed rest was very hard for me. I had to totally depend on my husband to do everything. He didn't have a problem with it, but I did, because I was so used to doing for him. This experience taught me how to be still and, how to receive help from others. Growing up without parents forced me to always do for myself. I didn't know how to receive help from anyone. I realized later that this was a form of *pride*. During that time

God showed me that I wasn't in this world by myself and that as long as I am here I will always need help from somebody. Also during this time my husband's job went on strike for three weeks. After two years into our marriage, we were hit financially from all sides. Both of us were out of work, and our money was getting very low. We both felt our situation appeared hopeless. During this time, we found ourselves praying and seeking God for guidance. We learned later that God allowed us to get into that situation, so we would seek Him. He knew He had work for us to do for His Kingdom. God knew the only way He could get our attention was to allow some thing to happen, where we would have to totally depend on Him. As we sought Him daily in our situation, we developed a personal relationship with Him. We started praying together every morning. We realized that if we sought God first, He would take care of all the rest.

"And he will give you all you need from day to day if you live for him and make the Kingdom of God your primary concern." (Matthew 6:33).

While I was out on bed rest, I pondered what we needed to do for the baby's arrival. We knew we weren't financially able, but we wanted to move into a bigger house before the baby was born. Now we are entering our first faith test.

2

SEEK GOD IN MARRIAGE

We talked with the realtor of our current house and learned that the house once belonged to his uncle. We discussed with him our desire to move. He told us that if we could move into another one of his houses, he could work out a trade off. Once again God gave us favor and showed Himself faithful. We moved into our new house in January and my baby Demarius was born in June. In September I would have to go back to work, but I didn't want to put my newborn baby in a daycare environment until he could talk. Our preference was for him to be kept by an older lady who could nurture him and give him that individual attention that all babies need. God showed us favor again! He led us to a very sweet lady, the mother of one of our friends. She kept Demarius until he was 2 years old, and she loved him and treated him as if he was her own. The going rate to keep a newborn baby at that time was about $135 per week, but she only charged us $50 per week (This blessing *was* God!). I went back to work with a peace, knowing that my child was in a safe place. We realized that God would take care of us in ways that we could never imagine and would give us the desires of our heart if we would only ask and trust Him. From that point on, we sought God *for* and *in* everything. As I continued to work as a Team Leader, thinking that I was not being paid what I was really worth, I learned that the focus was not about how much money I made or how many degrees I had. The key was how willing I was to position myself to learn all I could wherever I was, which would put me in a better position for other opportunities. I also learned that when a person decides to go to college, he/she should also discover his/her passion. That passion will lead them to the career path that they should pursue.

Notes

PART IV

HOW TO BE EFFECTIVE
AND
SUCCESSFUL IN YOUR
CAREER

1

WE CAN SERVE GOD
IN WHATEVER JOB WE HAVE

During my career, I noticed that God was setting me apart for some type of service for Him. Some of us think that in order to serve God we must preach, teach, or hold some other religious position in the church. That's not true at all. The purpose of pastors and teachers are to train the children of God in their individual gifting/calling and to send them out to make disciples wherever they go. We all can serve God, right where we are, in whatever occupations we have. ANY WORK we do – as a parent, artist, accountant, waiter, waitress, beautician, secretary, manager, doctor, lawyer, astronaut, housekeeper, teacher, banker, cook, athlete, scientist, truck driver, producer, veterinarian, etc. -- we should do it as unto the Lord.

"And whatever you do or say, let it be as a representative of the Lord Jesus, all the while giving thanks through Him to God the Father." (Col. 3:17).

As long as we are doing our work as unto the Lord, our work will represent Him. God has gifted all of us with different gifts/talents to use for His Glory.

"For God's gifts and his call can never be withdrawn." (Romans 11:29).

We can't work to earn His gifts. We should use our gifts/talents to build God's Kingdom and to give Him all the Glory. **Remember, only what we do for Christ will last.**

2

NEVER BE A PEOPLE PLEASER

I felt God's hand on me when I started losing interest in the activities I used to do and the places I used to go. When friends would ask me to go places or participate in certain activities, it didn't seem to fit anymore. Whenever I tried to participate I started feeling very uncomfortable and out of place. I didn't know what was going on. Even if I wanted to leave certain places, I didn't, because I was afraid of what someone would say about me. (I was a people pleaser). I worried about what everyone said about everything I did. I wanted to be liked by everybody. This battle lasted through high school, college, and then into the working world. The more I felt I didn't fit, the more I started questioning what was going on with me. God began to show me that He was equipping me with a gift for His use, and therefore, He was the only one that I needed to please. He wanted me to use this gift to encourage my friends, family, co-workers and community. In order for me to accomplish this task, He had to separate me from certain activities and places to make my witness for Him more effective. Sometimes when God eventually wants you to minister to a person that you spent countless hours with, you become very familiar with that person, and when that happens it becomes more difficult getting that individual to receive what you have to say. (Jesus had a similar challenge-- Because his community knew Him as the carpenter's son, they found it difficult to believe what God was doing through Him).

"He's just a carpenter's son, and we know Mary, his mother, and his brothers—James, Joseph, Simon, and Judas. All his sisters live right here among us. What makes him so great?" And they were deeply offended and refused to believe in him. Then Jesus told them, "A prophet is honored everywhere except in his own hometown and among his own family." (Matthew 13:55-57).

I then understood why God told us to be the "salt of the earth."

"You are the salt of the earth. But what good is salt if it has lost its flavor? Can you make it useful again? It will be thrown out and trampled underfoot as worthless." (Matthew 5:13).

We should try our best to live a Holy and consecrated life. That doesn't mean that we should be perfect by keeping a list of activities that we cannot do. It does mean however, that in order to be an example for Christ, we should strive for maturity by avoiding anything that is against God's Will. As Paul said,

"When I am with the Jews, I become one of them so that I can bring them to Christ. When I am with those who follow the Jewish laws, I do the same, even though I am not subject to the law, so that I can bring them to Christ. When I am with the Gentiles who do not have the Jewish law, I fit in with them as much as I can. In this way, I gain their confidence and bring them to Christ. But I do not discard the law of God; I obey the law of Christ. When I am with those who are oppressed, I share their oppression so that I might bring them to Christ. Yes, I try to find common ground with everyone so that I might bring them to Christ. I do all this to spread the

Good News, and in doing so I enjoy its blessings." (1 Cor. 9:20-23).

We should be living epistles. People should recognize Christ in us by the way we live, not just by what we say. God said you will know my children by their fruit. As I continued to work in the corporate world, my purpose was starting to unfold. I noticed that people, in all positions and from all walks of life, came to me to discuss their problems (work related and personal). After talking with a few people, God showed me through their situations that our struggles normally become strongholds because we use the wrong methods to solve them. We try to solve spiritual problems with carnal/worldly methods. He let me know that in order to help them, I would have to use spiritual methods (His biblical principles: The Word). At that point, I made a habit of reading His Word daily. He showed me that most, but not all, of our issues/struggles normally come from a deep rooted problem that started when we were young. And, because we never addressed the problem, the issue became an unbroken generational curse. Someone has to break that curse or we will pass the crisis down to the next generation. When I started reading the word, I noticed that each day, what I read would be related to me or someone I would come in contact with that same day. That fact really amazed me. I got excited and felt lost if I missed a day of reading. We must realize that just like we need a map to help us travel in this world, we need the Bible to help us live in this world. God showed me that in order to help those people He would send, I'd have to stay in His word. Since that revelation, as God sent people to me, He gave me the word to give them about their situation. God was fulfilling his purpose in my life, but I didn't know how He would do it or what to call it. In each place I worked, God allowed me to minister to more and more people. Later on I felt I wanted to work closer to home so I could be closer to my children. I was offered a position as a Facilitator. This job, which paid $40,000 per year, was five minutes from my home and five minutes from my child's school. I took the position, but I was concerned about the hours because it was a third shift job. I had never worked third shift before, so this could be a challenge. After one month on this job, I found out that I was two months pregnant with my second child. I wondered if God really wanted me to work third shift with a two-year-old and now, a newborn. And because I had just started the job, I didn't know how my employer would receive this unexpected news. Each morning that I read God's word, God gave me confirmation to tell my employer about my situation. I trusted the fact that God knows everything and allow all things to happen for His purposes. I did eventually tell my employer and everything went well. Two months later, I went into premature labor and was put on bed rest (again) for five months. I was out of work again. God reminded me that if He took care of us when I was on bed rest with my first child, He would take care of us this time.

3

STEPPING OUT OF YOUR COMFORT ZONE

While I was out of work this time, God gave me a clearer picture of His purpose for me. He showed me in the book of Haggai how He was going to use me in the workplace.

"Be strong. . . and work. For I am with you." Judah's people had returned to worshiping God, and God had promised to bless their efforts. But it was time for them to work. We must be people of prayer, Bible study, and worship—but eventually we must get out and do what God has in mind for us. He wants to change the world through us. God has given you a job to do in the church, at your place of employment, and at home. The time has come to be strong and work because God is with you!" (Haggai 2:4 (NLT notes)).

Not knowing how, I simply said, "Use me anyway you want to." My baby Domineke was born in August 1998, and I returned to work in October. The same little lady who kept my first child nurtured Domineke as well; for the same price.

My new born didn't take a bottle too well, so I had to nurse him -- every two hours. I didn't think I would be able to accommodate nursing my son, since I was on third shift, But God gave me favor with my employer, once again. I was able to go home during the night and nurse my child. (That was God's doing!). They allowed me to do this until he was weaned. As time passed, I found working third shift was becoming a challenge. In order to be an effective mother, I needed a first shift job. God showed me His order of community (God, family, then other interests). On August 29, 1999, I read the Word as usual, and my scripture translation read, "Sometimes God will ask us to step out into a job that seems like a demotion, but it will bring promotion in Him." I thought, prayed, and talked with my husband about this. God showed me that while our children were small, third shift was not where I needed to be. I needed to rearrange my priorities. My husband supported my thoughts and encouraged me to talk with my boss about it. He said that because I was honoring God's order, God would take care of us. (Thank God for an equally yoked husband!). The next day, I told my supervisor that I could no longer stay on third shift because it was interfering with my family's needs.

At that point, I thought I would lose my job because there were no openings at that time. God softened my employers' hearts to create a first shift job for me, but I had to take a $12,000 per year pay cut. My husband and I agreed that I should accept the position anyway because we knew God would supply whatever needs we had. Because God had helped us get through our previous struggles, we could trust Him yet again, to get us through the next ones. That's how our faith in Him continued to grow. When God told me to step out of my third shift job, He also told me that because of my obedience, according to a translated scripture in Luke, He would cancel our debt in a way that no one would understand. (We would experience a Year of Jubilee!!).

The Luke scripture read, "The scroll containing the messages of Isaiah the prophet was handed to him, and he unrolled the scroll to the place where it says: "The Spirit of the Lord is upon me, for he has appointed me to preach Good News to the poor. He has sent me to proclaim that captives will be released, that the blind will see, that the downtrodden will be freed from their oppressors, and that the time of the Lord's favor has come." He rolled up the scroll, handed it back to the attendant, and sat down. Everyone in the synagogue stared at him intently. Then he said, "This Scripture has come true today before your very eyes!" (Luke 4:17-21)

This revelation started a new dimension of faith for us. Our mortgage was $1,100 per month. For whatever reason, God did not allow my husband and me to calculate the lost income before I accepted the lower paying job. I guess God knew that we would've based our decision totally on our natural resources, instead of our spiritual resources. God made our situation a testimony for His Glory! After everything was calm, we decided to figure our income, and we realized that we would not have enough money for the mortgage. We didn't know how we were going to pay it. We immediately called the mortgage company to set up a payment plan, but they didn't have a plan available. We sent the mortgage company what we could. Since we knew we couldn't pay the full monthly amount, we decided to sell our house and move into a more economical place. We looked for another place, but nothing worked out. Months passed, and we continually sent the mortgage company what we could. We did this for about ten months, and then finally the mortgage company started asking for the remainder of their money and threatening foreclosure.

Notes

PART V

PROMOTION COMES
FROM GOD

1

GOD WILL GIVE YOU
FAVOR WITH MAN

In May 2000, we discussed our situation with our lawyer friend. She suggested that we file for bankruptcy. We didn't know too much about bankruptcy, but we were willing to look into it. She presented all options to us. We could file a Chapter 7 or a Chapter 13. With Chapter 7, our creditors wouldn't get anything, but if we filed Chapter 13, our creditors would get a little each month until they were paid in full. We could have easily filed Chapter 7, but our conscience reminded us of God's word:

"Pay all your debts, except the debt of love for others." (Romans 13:8).

Thus, we filed Chapter 13. One month after we filed bankruptcy, my employer offered me another position with more than a 40% increase. (That was nobody but God!). We went from August 1999 to June 2000 without paying our full mortgage payment each month. Even though we were willing to move and give up whatever we had, God allowed us to keep it all! He allowed us to keep the house, cars, furniture, plus created a job for me with a pay increase. While on that new assignment, God continued to send people to me for ministering, with different types of issues. People from the least to the greatest, (in employment status), would ask me to find scripture for them relating to their situation. I knew then that God wanted to use me in the workplace. Everyday I continued to pray, "Lord please use me in a position where I can advise/encourage people according to your biblical principles." I noticed when people talked about their issues, they became more focused and effective in whatever task they were trying to perform. No matter who we are in society or what positions we hold, we are still human beings with real issues. We must deal with those issues in order to be productive citizens.

2

BE AVAILABLE FOR GOD TO USE YOU

I finally realized why I felt so differently and never fit in with cliques (and still don't). God separated me from certain people and places so no one would speak evil of my name. Then people would trust that I would keep their concerns confidential. I now understand why certain situations happened in my life. After I prayed the prayer to "advise/encourage people," God continued to move me in that direction. The next week, after my prayer request, my cousin, showed me a pamphlet about a company that hires corporate Chaplains to talk with their employees once a week. The Chaplain meets with employees to discuss any emotional or spiritual issues they may have and provides resources to meet those needs. The Chaplain also prays for them, upon their request, and gives them scriptures related to their situation. I was shocked because this was exactly how God was using me. I was also amazed that such a service existed. This showed me that God orders our footsteps to fulfill the purpose that He has for our lives.

"Trust in the Lord with all your heart; do not depend on your own understanding. Seek his will in all you do, and he will direct your paths." (Proverbs 3:5-6).

Our gifts make room for us. Sometimes we get a little frustrated when we know God promises to do something in our lives, but our desire does not happen how and when we want it. We must realize that we receive our gifts and talents freely from God. He is responsible for when, where and how we use those gifts. God just wants our willing and available spirit when He calls. We shouldn't try to MAKE anything happen. Because we are all one body in Christ and we each have different gifts and talents to build His Kingdom, we should not be upset or jealous about anyone else's gift. We all have a specific gift/talent that will solve a specific problem and meet a specific need. God uses us according to His pleasure. When we try to accomplish a task other than the task God equips/calls us to do, we become unfruitful and unfulfilled. We are also ineffective if we do what we are *not* called to do. The ANOINTING is the only power that breaks yokes; therefore, we have to be in our RIGHT CALL in order to be used to deliver those people that God will send, according to the ANOINTED PURPOSE He has for us to fulfill. Normally our purpose is connected to a task that we "naturally" love to do and would do without pay.

3
GOD OPENS DOORS THAT NO MAN CAN CLOSE

After my cousin told me about the Chaplaincy Service, I decided to research the organization. I realized that this was exactly what I wanted to do full time. I enrolled in classes to pursue the Chaplain's certification. I took two classes and had to stop because I couldn't afford anymore classes at that time, but I hoped to return soon. All along, God continued to use me to advise/encourage people. One incident in particular confirmed that being a Workplace Chaplain was the call on my life. It happened when a supervisor had marriage problems, he asked Human Resources to page me to pray for him. This was my final confirmation that God was calling me to be a Chaplain in the Workplace. In December of 2001, I was laid off -- Yes, from the job that had just given me a promotion with a raise. I was a little puzzled until I remembered that nothing happens by coincidence. God allowed this to happen for a reason. I had to constantly remind myself of (Rev. 3:7) which states:

"This is the message from the one who is holy and true. He is the one who has the key of David. He opens doors, and no one can shut them; he shuts doors, and no one can open them."

So during the time I was laid off, I used that time to learn more about Chaplaincy and to spend more time with my family. My youngest son was four at that time, and my oldest son was six. Being home allowed me to volunteer at my oldest son's school and prepare my youngest son for kindergarten. As I waited for God to open another door for me, I focused my attention on what I could do for my family. A few months later, my husband brought me an application from a business that he was familiar with. Their Material Expediter did not return to work, therefore, her position was open and the manager wanted to fill it as soon as possible. I filled out the application and sent it back through my husband on a Wednesday. I went for an interview on Thursday, they offered me the job on Friday, and I started work the following Monday (That was God!). My total benefit package was higher than the one I had at the previous job. How quickly I got this job showed me that whatever door God wants to open, it will open. When I began this job, God used me to encourage those co-workers as well. I encouraged whomever He sent. At this time I prayed to be able to put my four-year-old in a structured preschool, which would prepare him for Kindergarten. After I prayed, a cousin told me about a program for four year olds called the More at Four Program. This was a free program to prepare children for kindergarten. I didn't think we would qualify, but I applied anyway. My son was accepted into the program. (That was nobody but God!) He attended a Montessori school FREE until he enrolled in kindergarten. I saw even more that God controlled everything. My faith continued to grow stronger. God allows things to happen in a way that we could never understand. He orchestrates events in order to give us the desires of our hearts and to fulfill His purpose for our lives. My youngest son started kindergarten and my husband and I continued to experience the hand of God move in our situations.

A short time later we had car problems, and we needed a vehicle. Even though we knew we were currently in bankruptcy, we went looking for a vehicle anyway. We knew that God would supply our needs no matter what our financial situation. Our two vehicles were 14 years old, so we definitely needed a vehicle. As we looked for a car, God led us to a place that allowed us to purchase a vehicle despite our circumstances. That same year, we found a finance company that paid off the bankruptcy loan, both of the first and second mortgage lenders in full, and refinanced our house at a lower interest rate. (That was God!) He paid all our debt just like He promised (Luke 4:17-21). And, we were also discharged from bankruptcy.

4
NEVER GIVE UP ON YOUR DREAMS

In November 2004, I called to register for Chaplaincy classes again, but the program had been discontinued by this time. They referred me to another Chaplaincy program, which I had never heard of. This program hires Chaplains to serve in businesses all over the United States. I contacted them, completed their application, and completed their interview by phone and e-mail. In January 2005, they offered me an On-Call Marketplace Chaplain position for the Research Triangle Park, NC area. My workplace experience and testimonials throughout my life qualified me for the position. I accepted the position with *awe* at what God had done. God had manifested His call for my life-- a *"Chaplain in the Workplace"*, in His way and in His timing. He had A*nointed* and A*ppointed* me *"For Such a Time as This.* He is *so faithful.*

After all June and I went through, God has continued to lead people to us who are going through some of the same situations. After hearing our story, they claim the hope that God will fulfill His purpose/call on their life, no matter what they go through. Our testimony builds their faith to keep on pressing on. We should not let people discourage us from what we know God has said. If we had listened to the negative things people said, we would never have gotten through our circumstances. People offered such discouraging words as "You have to have a degree to do this or that" or "If you file bankruptcy, you won't be able to get this or that." Thank God we didn't listen. When you walk by *faith* please remember to choose your *advisors* carefully. Our situation allowed God the opportunity to work through the impossible and get *ALL* the *GLORY!!!!* When MAN says no, look for God to show up and show *OUT!!* Thank God we did not give up and quit. We must realize that who we are is not determined by our struggles or circumstances. Who we are is determined by how we *RESPOND* to our circumstances. Going through our struggles with a peace and trust in God makes us more effective witnesses for *HIM*. This blessed peace also gives God the opportunity to make our life a message of Hope for someone else.

Notes

PART VI

TIME TO USE YOUR GOD GIVEN TALENTS AND GIFTS

1

THIS IS THE ULTIMATE QUESTION:

"DO YOU *TRUST* WHO YOU *PROFESS* OR WHAT YOU *POSSESS?*"

According to God's Word, we must give an account of our lives.

"Yes, each of us will have to give a personal account to God." (Romans 14:12).

We must explain how we used our time, gifts, and talents. All of us are servants of God. The Holy Spirit equips us to serve him. God gives each of us -- young, old, educated, uneducated, rich or poor -- gifts and talents to use to build His Kingdom. These gifts should be used to fulfill His purpose for our lives.

"God has given gifts to each of you from his great variety of spiritual gifts. Manage them well so that God's generosity can flow through you." (1 Peter 4:10).

Notes

PART VII

FEARS THAT HINDER
FULFILLING YOUR DREAMS

There are three common FEARS which hinder us from fulfilling our purpose, (rejection, limited resources and inadequacy). We must remember,

"For God has not given us a spirit of fear and timidity, but of power, love, and self-discipline." (2 Tim. 1:7) "That is why we live by believing and not by seeing." (2 Corin. 5:7). "So, you see, it is impossible to please God without faith. Anyone who wants to come to him must believe that there is a God and that he rewards those who sincerely seek him." (Hebrews 11:6).

Now let's look at those Fears……

1

FEAR OF REJECTION

Rejection should not hinder us because God, who knew us before we entered our mother's womb, called and predestined us before the foundation of the earth said, -

"I knew you before I formed you in your mother's womb. Before you were born I set you apart and appointed you as my spokesman to the world." (Jeremiah 1:5)   "But you belong to God, my dear children. You have already won your fight with these false prophets, because the Spirit who lives in you is greater than the spirit who lives in the world."
(1 John 4:4).

God uses the foolish things of this world to confound the wise.
 "He opens doors, and no one can shut them; he shuts doors, and no one can open them."
(Rev. 3:7).

2

FEAR OF LIMITED RESOURCES

God is our Source.

"The earth is the Lord's, and everything in it. The world and all its' people belong to him." (Psalm 24:1). For all the animals of the forest are mine, and I own the cattle on a thousand hills." (Psalm 50:10). "The silver is mine, and the gold is mine, says the Lord Almighty." (Haggai 2:8).

He gives us good health and strength to use our hands to work each day and obtain a paycheck for our labor. He uses people to help each other. We are supposed to be channels for each other, not reservoirs. God blesses us to be a blessing. God will use whoever he chooses to bless us. We should treat everyone the way we want to be treated because sometimes we entertain angels and don't even realize it. *The person that you hate could be the person God uses to bless you.*

(SELAH!)   Forgiveness opens the door for God's unexpected resources.

3

FEAR OF INADEQUACY

When we feel that we aren't educated or qualified enough, we must remember that man may choose the most educated, but God educates the *CHOSEN*. There's nothing wrong with obtaining degrees because that training is a form of preparation. But God can still use us without the degrees. On every job assignment, we should work as if God is our supervisor. If we work on our jobs as unto the Lord, God will give us favor with the people on our jobs. We should take the initiative to learn all we can. Also, we should be willing to do more than is expected of us. Doing more gives us more experience, and this knowledge positions us for promotion. Promotion does not come from man - - it comes from God. We must work as unto the Lord and know that He will reward us.

"And whatever you do or say, let it be as a representative of the Lord Jesus, all the while giving thanks through him to God the Father." (Col. 3:17).

By doing more than is expected, we build an indirect resume for God, who equips and qualifies us for the next available opportunity.

The resume is the most common tool used in society to determine a person's worth. Let's compare man's resume to God's......

PART VIII

MAN'S -VS- GOD'S RESUME

MAN'S RESUME	GOD'S RESUME
Education: College or Institution	**Education:** School of the Holy Spirit
Objective: To pursue degrees to get a job paying lots of money so we can get the items we want.	**Objective:** To pursue God's call for our life and to be fruitful and fulfilled, by using His gifts and talents to build His Kingdom (only by His favor, grace, and mercy, through His son Jesus Christ).
Experience: Different places where we've worked.	**Experience:** Trials and tribulations we've been through that will be a testimony to help others.
Achievements: Work hard to obtain money, fame, and recognition	**Achievements:** Do all our work as unto the Lord, and He will reward us. Our gift will make room for us.
References: List of people who have known us most of our career	**References:** God who knew us before we were formed in our mother's womb and said, "He who began a good work in us, will be faithful to complete it"
Letter of Recommendation: Letters from our past employers and peers, highlighting our strengths and potential	**Letter of Recommendation:** The souls saved because of our testimony of how God used us in spite of our weaknesses and circumstances.
Degree: Associates, Bachelor's, Master's or Doctorate	**Degree:** God's approval for enduring life, waiting to hear him say, "Well done thy good and faithful servant."

Conclusion

God allows trials to build our character and patience. He allows this to better equip us to serve in this world in the capacity that He desires for His Glory. The awesome fact about this task is that when we truly walk in God's call for our lives, we will be fruitful and fulfilled. We will also get rewarded for something we have a passion to do. We help others while giving God all the Glory and all the Praise.

Notes

Comments

One of the things that we need in the body, are stories of victory from people who are not a part of the Five Fold Ministry. When someone who is not a full time minister, or a preacher or teacher, decides to believe in the priesthood of every believer, and then shares their vision, insight, and story, it is so powerful. It offers a level of encouragement that is almost too wonderful to imagine. It causes everyday people to realize that God cares about their everyday problems, and moves in the ordinary for ordinary people, but in an extraordinary way. And this book is exactly that type of story, and I would recommend it to anyone who is wondering if God is really there, and if He really cares. It is a blessing.

-Andy Thompson
Senior Pastor, World Overcomers Christian Church,
Durham, North Carolina

Your book is a powerful message that will touch the lives of many people. It brings hope and real meaning to those of us who have lost a loved one and experienced adversities in life. It allows us to connect with our deepest feelings and appreciate having the opportunity to grow and obtain wisdom through our experiences.

-Sylvia C. Bittle
School Principal, Durham, North Carolina

I feel so honored to have had the privilege to read "The Struggle with a Purpose". In a time where there's much uncertainty about your purpose in life, this book brings such clarity on the subject. I also believe that "The Struggle with a Purpose" is a must-read for anyone who has ever been in or is now in the midst of their own personal struggle, it gives you simple guidelines as to how to go through your pain knowing there is hope on the other side. "The Struggle with a Purpose" was written with a unique balance of excellence and practicality that will bless the masses. As a close friend of Minister McNeill, I am a witness of some of the victories she has experienced because of her faith and trust in God. You too can experience those same victories as you apply these principles to your life.

-Cheryl Blue
Co-Pastor, Word of Truth Christian Center, Vass, North Carolina

It has been said that to have a true testimony, you must experience some test in life. Leslie McNeill's tests have resulted in a testimony that is inspiring. Mrs. McNeill takes you on a journey of faith and favor that ebbs and flows and proves that God in his ultimate wisdom allows test to beset our lives so that we become billboards for his glory. This work shares the test of life with praise, thanksgiving and humility. Prayerfully it will enable you to claim your victory and boldly proclaim to the world the power of a God given testimony.

-Dana G. Jones,
Attorney at Law, Durham, North Carolina

When I finished reading this book I realized that it was written for those who refused to waste another day, hour, minute, and who desires to increase momentum, and maximize every single day. This book should and will encourage others that through your struggles (Leslie), their best is yet to come. Even though you went through struggles, you were always working on a way out, whether it was just having faith in God or just not giving up. Before you even met God you were a fighter and now you are a warrior.

-Wendy Major,

White as Snow Cleaning Services, Durham, North Carolina

Leslie McNeill is BRILLANT!   This book is a living testimony as to how one can rise up from the adversity of struggle and use his/her struggle as a mechanism to encourage, motivate, and infuse change into the lives of others.   I pray that this is the first of many more great works we will receive from her.

-Lorenzo Roberts,
Accounting Services, Durham, North Carolina

About the Author

Leslie Annette McNeill was raised on a farm in a small town, in North Carolina, called Wagram, which is near Laurinburg, NC. She's married to John W. McNeill Jr., a Music Producer, who is also from Wagram. They have two children: Demarius and Domineke. She holds two Bachelor of Science degrees; Manufacturing Technology (Major) and Automotive Technology (Minor), from North Carolina A&T State University, where she graduated cum laude. She is an On-Call Marketplace Chaplain, (for the Research Triangle Park, NC area), for Marketplace Ministries, in Dallas, TX. She has worked in various fields, in Corporate America, for over seventeen years. Leslie is very passionate about spending time with her family and encouraging others. She wrote this book in an effort to inspire and motivate others to maximize their full potential, by fulfilling their God designed purpose. To contact Leslie, write:

Leslie A. McNeill
PO Box 72653
Durham, NC 27712
Email: mcneillleslie@yahoo.com
www.amazon.com